GEMS AND JEWELS

UNCUT STONES AND OBJETS D'ART

With an introduction by Henri-Jean Schubnel

CRESCENT BOOKS

Contents

Acknowledgments are due to the following for photographs used in this volume:

Carlo Bevilacqua: 1-4, 6-10, 15, 16, 18, 19, 23, 24, 29, 30, 33-38, 40, 43-55, 58, 59, 62, 65-129
Bibliothèque Nationale, Paris: 11, 14, 17, 31
Crown Copyright, by permission of the Controller, HMSO: 27, 28, 60
De Beer: 56, 57
Rapho-Fathy: 5
Scala: 12, 13, 20, 22, 25, 26, 32
Smithsonian Institution, Washington: 63, 64
Van Cleef & Arpels: 61
Versailles, photographic library: 21, 39, 41, 42

Translated from the French by Henri-Jean Schubnel

Gemmology, the science of gemstones, is rather more than just a branch of mineralogy. It also helps us to understand one of the most important aspects of the history of mankind: the relationship between man and those remarkable mineral substances which, because of their beauty, durability and rarity, are an integral part of his history. Charged with significance of which he may be only partly aware, they have helped him to overcome his fears and pains in the face of events that pass his understanding.

Even the rational explanation of what many people consider superstition or, more charitably, 'popular belief' cannot take away from the poetry and romance of traditions which are many thousands of years old; it only serves to show us how the human race, throughout its infancy and adolescence, has sought to protect itself behind the walls of mysticism, whose stones are those that can be easily carried, and easily hidden.

There is a close parallel between the talisman or amulet of ancient man and the jewelry of modern times; it is only the symbolic values that have altered. Today, the concept of invoking superhuman forces has been replaced by a belief which survives all religions and all civilisations: the belief in money. Money, the spirit within all those material substances that modern man loves to watch growing, shrinking, changing shape; rejecting all symbolic values that rise from the collective subconscious in favour of the practical worth of the physical object. And so, redeeming man from ruin and despair, precious stones remain, as always, the talismans of power.

Henri-Jean Schubnel
Technical director, Association française de gemmologie

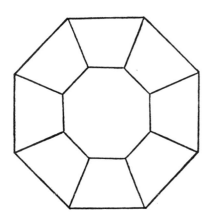
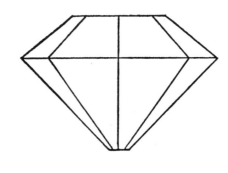
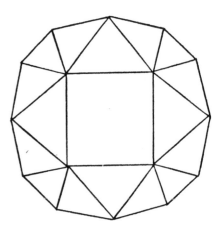

Historical introduction

The long history of gemstones and their use is lost in the mists of time. Before the dawn of history, our oldest ancestors sought out all sorts of stones which, because of their solidity and hardness, could be used to make the necessary tools and weapons for everyday life. The stoneworker's craft, therefore, is much older than that which we have come to call jewelry – a separate and complex art that has evolved gradually from the beginning of historic times to the present day.

At the beginning of the Neolithic age, men could already distinguish certain sparkling or richly-coloured stones to which they attributed supernatural powers; powers that they believed they could enhance by the engraving of magic signs. So, by the end of prehistoric times, such stones had become the first established medium of exchange between the desert nomads and the settled farming communities. Valued for their magical properties rather than their beauty, these gems were not articles of luxury but everyday necessities.

In Sumer, engraved gems became the first seals, for it was believed that in certain cases the stone could pass on its magic power. By means of the sign that one imprinted on the clay tablet, the object itself was placed under the protection of powerful forces, which would drive off thieves and other misfortunes; it was only much later that the seal was used as a signature. Made of quartz, onyx or other semiprecious stone, these seals were in the shape of buttons or rough hemispheres engraved in intaglio, or sometimes in the form of a cylinder, pierced along its axis of rotation so that it could be worn on a string about the neck.

To begin with, the use of amulets was particularly widespread in Egypt, and the vast number of scarabs, figures and religious symbols engraved on gems that have been discovered there show that this art could equal that of Egyptian statuary in the virtuosity of its execution. We can get some idea of the extent of the commerce in gems from the spread of these indestructible little objects, and without doubt the demand for them in distant countries was one of the most important factors in the spread of civilisation. We know that the Sumerian civilisation extended as far as the valley of the Indus; and Assyrian cylinder-seals and tablets have been discovered in the Caucasus. Ornamental stones like the lapis lazuli of Afghanistan were already being used 6000 years ago, and since it is almost certain that this was the only source known at that time, it is very surprising to find these stones not only in burial mounds on the coasts of the Baltic Sea (where one also finds amber) but in the tombs of Morocco. For more widely-distributed stones it is, of course, difficult to be sure of their origins, and so impossible to map their movements in the trade of ancient times.

Certain gemstones have excited the admiration of people from very different civilisations. In China, jade was valued higher than any other stone, and has been worked from 2000 BC to the present day; and in Mexico, jade and turquoise were more sought-after by the ancient Mayas than gold. Some gemstones, such as cornelian, found favour with all prehistoric peoples: this stone, in pierced round or oval shapes, has been found in very many places far removed from archeological excavations; it has even been discovered in Siberia, at Durdanskaya and Akcha, where it was worked in Mesolithic times, together with other chalcedonies and jaspers of various colours, in very delicate flakes.

It is particularly difficult to determine the order of appearance of different gems in history. One can be sure that jade and various quartzes were in use for the manufacture of tools in prehistoric times; that lapis lazuli, obsidian, cornelian, agate and jasper were cut and engraved in Sumerian times, in the shape of beads, seals, amulets, cups, flowers and little figures of animals. In Egypt, it is malachite that one finds first of all in tombs (the Egyptians used powdered malachite to colour their eyelids); then lapis lazuli and obsidian; later cornelian, jasper, amethyst, turquoise and amazon-stone; and only much later emerald, aquamarine, hematite, garnets, amber, coral and pearl. The Bible makes frequent references to gems, and the prophet

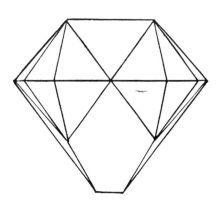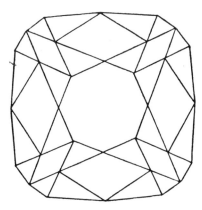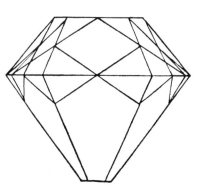

The development of the brilliant cut for diamonds. Left to right: the original 'eight cut' introduced during the fourteenth century, which is now only used for very small stones; the 'sixteen cut', also known as the Mazarin after the famous French cardinal whose stones were cut in this fashion; and the first brilliant cut perfected by Vincenzo Peruzzi at the end of the seventeenth century

Ezekiel described the robe of Hiram of Tyre (10th century BC) as follows: 'Every precious stone was thy covering, the sardius, topaz, and the diamond, the beryl, the onyx, and the jasper, the sapphire, the emerald, and the carbuncle, and gold'. In all probability, the 'sapphires' were lapis lazuli, and the 'carbuncles' almandine garnets.

Towards the end of the Assyrian empire very many gems were in circulation, and they were valued as much for their rarity and beauty as for their workmanship. In Greece, on the other hand, the material was of less importance, and the cutting of cameos and intaglios reached a perfection only equalled by certain engravers of the Renaissance. The name of the engraver Pyrgoteles has been immortalised by the many portraits of Alexander the Great which he cut in gems. A little later in time, the city of Alexandria became the most important centre for the manufacture of cameos; it was probably there that the two most remarkable examples of ancient gem-carving were made: the cup of Ptolemy and the magnificent Farnese plate (illustration 12), which must have taken twenty or thirty years to complete. A third internationally-known masterpiece, the 'Great Cameo' (illustration 14), was made by Dioskorides during the first century AD in Rome, which was already overflowing with jewels and cameos. Remarkably, however, the Romans knew nothing of the incomparable and subtle beauty of the cut diamond and, like the Greeks, employed this rarest of stones only for its hardness in cutting other gems.

As with all the other arts, gem-engraving followed Rome into its decline, and in Europe only Byzantium preserved, for nearly ten centuries, the secrets of the art. At the same time it remained flourishing in Persia, India and China, and Arab sailors feverishly sought out all kinds of gems. In the 9th century they ventured as far as Madagascar to obtain quartz, which they then sold throughout the East. From the beginning of the 16th century there was a particular demand for cut rock-crystal – of which the Renaissance has left us so many outstanding examples – and European traders in their turn began to exploit the Madagascar deposits.

Europe itself produced few gems of value. Nevertheless, a rock-crystal of great purity was obtained in the Alps; Bohemia yielded the celebrated pyrope garnet (the 'Arizona ruby'), Spain produced jet and Germany agate, and from the Massif Central in France came amethyst and a sapphire that the mediaeval alchemists pronounced as inferior only to those that came from the Indies. The rarest and most beautiful precious stones came from Ceylon and India, where the art of fashioning them had been practised from antiquity; but in these countries they knew nothing of regular cutting, contenting themselves with polishing the natural faces of crude crystals and adding facets on the circumference of precious stones, while attempting to reduce their weight as little as possible. The practice of cutting precious stones to regular forms, and the development of the techniques of diamond cutting, were established in Europe.

The method of splitting a diamond so as to obtain the natural regular octahedral form was known in Gaul and in Germany. About 1380 a true cutting technique was practised in France: a large flat face (the table) was made by cutting across one of the apexes of the octahedron; then the 'ribs' of this table and those on the back of the stone were cut to give eight supplementary facets. In 1475 Charles Le Témeraire, Duke of Burgundy, entrusted three large diamonds (one of which was known later as the Sancy diamond) to Louis de Berquem for cutting. He cut them so outstandingly that the fashion of using facetted diamonds for jewelry was soon adopted by the French royal court, and at once imitated in other European courts. Because of this, tradition has named Louis de Berquem the father of modern diamond-cutting, because he developed the 32-facet cut, using a horizontal steel grinding-wheel covered with diamond powder suspended in oil. A century later, Vincenzo Peruzzi perfected the 56-facet cut which, thanks to the perfection made possible by the mechanisation of the grinding wheel, has become the modern 'brilliant cut'.

The rebirth of the art of gem engraving took place in Italy in the fifteenth century, and it was under the influence of

5

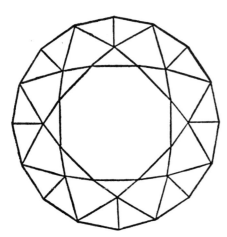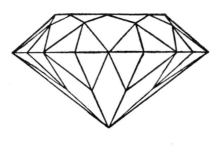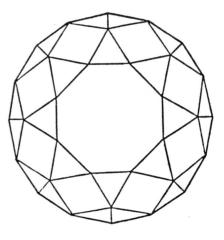

the Medici collection, the finest assembly of antique engraved gems and other works of art, that fifteenth and sixteenth century engravers succeeded in creating masterpieces worthy of the greatest engravers of antiquity. Like other Italian artists, they were much sought after by foreign rulers, and several agreed to leave their native country: the Miseronis for the court of Emperor Rudolph II, Benvenuto Cellini and Matteo de Nazzaro for that of François I.

At this time, there was still strong belief in the mystic powers and medicinal virtues of gems, a belief that the Middle Ages had themselves inherited from antiquity – and one that has, even today, not quite disappeared: there is, for instance, the common belief in birthstones, derived no doubt from cabalistic writings. In this short work it is impossible to enlarge on the varying significance of precious stones, and the virtues or baleful powers that man has attributed to them since the dawn of history; we are concerned solely with their use for personal adornment or ornamentation.

Between the sixteenth and nineteenth centuries three outstanding events dominated the history of gemmology: the colonisation of Latin America by the Spanish, who exported many very beautiful emeralds; the discovery of diamonds in Brazil in 1723, and the consequent loss to India of the monopoly in their production; and the later discovery of the rich diamond deposits in South Africa in 1867, which made the diamond accessible for the first time to a large number of people.

A sign of the times is the appearance on the market, since the end of the last century, of artificial or synthetic stones, which have gone to swell the already large quantity of false stones produced in the attempt to imitate real precious stones. Like copies and reproductions of works of art, they show only a slight resemblance to the imitated object, and can never recapture its charm and subtle personality. And in the case of precious stones: when one bears in mind the vast geological eras they have survived, and their ages measured in hundreds of millions of years, imitation stones by comparison are merely ridiculous.

Classification of principal gems and gemstones

It has become customary during the present century to divide gems into various categories, such as: precious stones, semi-precious stones and ornamental stones. Round about 1880, the following were considered as precious stones: diamond, corundum, ruby (spinel at that time was also known as Balas Ruby), emerald, sapphire, amethyst, agate, aventurine, garnet, lapis lazuli, opal, topaz and turquoise. Nowadays the tendency is to divide the minerals used in jewelry into two categories: gems, when the stone is mounted in a setting; and ornamental stones, which are an actual part of the manufactured precious object. The term precious stone is reserved for the diamond and for the various forms of corundum – ruby, sapphire and diamond.

Clearly, at some time or other it will be necessary to restrict the number of mineral species that can properly be called gems, since more than a thousand can be cut and polished. It would be logical to include all the traditional gems and ornamental stones, but to inspect with care the great profusion of cut minerals announced in various publications on the subject.

The order of classification given here corresponds to that of mineralogy, and takes account of the chemical composition and molecular structure of each gem. Non-crystalline minerals, and substances of non-mineral origin, will be dealt with separately.

Pure elements

DIAMOND. Pure carbon crystallising in the cubic system (strictly a mixture of two allotropes of carbon).

Known in India since at least 1000 BC, the diamond is the hardest of all minerals: it takes its name from two Greek words – *diaphanes*, transparent, and *adamas*, which at first meant extremely hard and now itself means diamond. The most perfect diamonds are without any fault or variation of

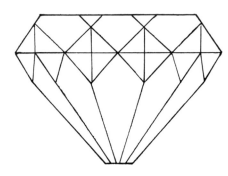
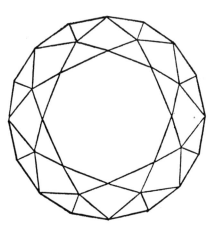
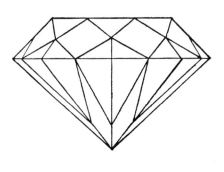

colour, yellowness or brownishness, which renders them less valuable. Some rare stones are golden-yellow, or pale pink, blue-green or red; the clear colours are much sought after, particularly those of a blue-whiteness.

The diamond is the most important of precious stones: by itself it represents as much as 80% of the trade in gems, and (taking into account the production of industrial diamonds which cannot be used in jewelry on account of their opacity or bad colour) ranks 19th in world mineral production. In 1965, 32 million carats of stones were mined throughout the world, of which 7.12 million were used in jewelry; the previous year this figure was 6.97 million. By 1968, the world production of diamonds had risen to over 43 million carats per year.

Of all the cuts, the brilliant cut is the most often used, since this makes the most of the refraction colours that are the particular charm of this stone. Diamond cutting is complicated by the variations in hardness that are met according to the angle of the faces in relation to the axis of the crystal. The stone may only be scratched or cut by another diamond, or worked with diamond powder.

The rock which is the source of diamonds is kimberlite, a basic lava which forms the famous diamond-bearing 'pipes' as it blocks volcanic chimneys caused by explosions below the earth's crust. Diamonds are also found in pre-Cambrian conglomerates, in grits, and most often in fairly old and redistributed alluvium (such as river sedimentation, marine shelves or sandbanks). From the Indian deposits, which were the sole source of diamonds until the 18th century, some two tons (10 million carats) were obtained, although the present production is no more than 2,000 carats a year. At the present time it is estimated that the known sources, added to the total of stones already extracted, make up scarcely 200 tons, even when industrial diamonds are included. Annual world production of more than 100,000 carats of diamonds for jewelry is attained by thirteen countries: South Africa, Botswana, Angola, Sierra Leone, Tanzania, Congo Republic (Brazzaville), Liberia, Zaïre Republic (Kinshasa), Ghana, USSR, Central African Republic, Brazil, the Ivory Coast and British Guiana.

Some of the most famous diamonds:
Cullinan (3,106 carats uncut). Found in the Premier mine, South Africa, in 1905, and cut into 105 separate stones of which one, of 530 carats, is the principal stone of the British royal sceptre.
Excelsior (995 carats uncut). Found in the Jägersfontein mine in South Africa, 1893.
President Vargas (726 carats uncut). Found at Rio San Antonio in Brazil in 1938, and cut into 29 stones, the largest of which is 48 carats.
Regent (420 carats uncut). Found at Partial in India in 1701, and reduced to a single stone of 137 carats by successful cutting. It is now in the Louvre in Paris.
Orloff. Found in India at Kollur, and bought for Catherine II at the end of the 18th century. Cut weight 199 carats.
Koh-i-nor. Indian stone known since 1304; its cut weight was 186, but it was re-cut in 1852 to a stone of 108 carats.
Hope. The 'Blue diamond' of 112 carats uncut weight was found in India at Kollur, bought by Louis XIV in 1668, and cut to a weight of 67 carats. It was stolen in 1792 and re-cut; the Hope diamond (44 carats) of the Smithsonian Institution is probably this stone.

Sulphides

PYRITE. Iron sulphide (cubic). Sometimes used for inexpensive jewelry, and often known as 'marcasite'. The beauty of the crystals, with their pale yellow metallic lustre, makes this a mineral in demand for decoration.

CHALCOPYRITE. Sulphide of copper and iron (tetragonal). Sometimes used in inexpensive jewelry; its appearance is similar to that of pyrite.

Halides

FLUORITE. Calcium fluoride (cubic); frequently known as fluorspar. One of the minerals used by man since prehistoric times, and discovered in the Upper Paleolithic. It is rarely cut in facets because it splits easily, but it is often employed

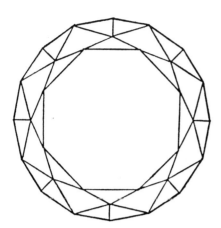
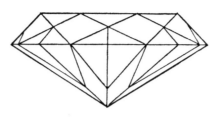
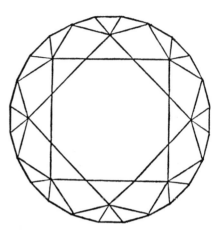

in ornamentation, although its softness is a disadvantage; it has been worked in China for a very long time. It occurs in a variety of colours: pink, yellow, violet, blue, green etc., often in hydrothermal lodes or in other kinds of deposit. The polychrome green and violet forms are particularly sought after.

Oxides

SPINEL. Magnesium aluminium oxide (cubic). Beautiful spinels are highly valued, and some of them have been taken for rubies or sapphires. Found in many different colours – pink, red, violet, orange, blue or brown – spinels are typical contact metamorphic crystals, frequently found in alluvium. The best stones come from Ceylon, Burma and India, and most of the great 'rubies' of history are in reality red spinels; this is the case with three of the most famous: the Black Prince and Timur rubies of the British crown jewels, and the Côte de Bretagne in the Paris Louvre.

CHRYSOBERYL. Beryllium aluminium oxide (orthorhombic). Generally yellow in colour, as the prefix *chryso,* Greek for gold, suggests. Chrysoberyl has two particularly interesting varieties: cat's eye or chymophane, in which the cabochon cut brings out a special iridescence in the form of a luminous silvery band between two coloured zones, yellow and pale green; and the very rare and valuable alexandrite. Discovered in 1831 at Takowaya in the Urals, on the day when Czar Alexander II attained his majority, alexandrite is emerald green in daylight, but dark red in artificial light.

Chrysoberyl and its varieties occur in acid rocks or where they are in contact with micaschists or dolomitic marbles, and in alluvium. The best alexandrites come from the Urals; large stones are also found in Ceylon, together with cat's eye, and yellowish-green and pale green-yellow chrysoberyl. Some sources in Africa and Brazil yield interesting yellow or green crystals. Generally speaking, Ceylon alexandrite is not as beautiful as the Russian stone, which often surpasses the sapphire in beauty and value.

CORUNDUM. Aluminium oxide (trigonal). Although the many varieties of this stone are widespread, transparent crystals of good colour are rare and much sought-after. Known in India from the beginning of historic times, they occur in a wide range of colours: from the rosy-pink to the dark red of the ruby, through the spectrum of colour to the blue and violet of the sapphire. With the exception of the ruby, all the coloured varieties are commonly given the name of sapphire, whether white or golden, pink or green. Unlike the diamond, the corundum does not diminish in value when small inclusions are present, provided that these flaws are not too visible.

As in the case of other gems, these inclusions are in fact of help in the distinction of natural stones from valueless synthetic corundum. Corundums sometimes exhibit the phenomenon of asterism (a six-rayed star); this is caused by the presence in the stone of a lattice of fine needles of rutile. Star rubies and sapphires are always given the cabochon cut so as to show the star to best advantage; it appears to shimmer across the surface of the stone at the least movement.

There are many sources of corundums, but those of gem quality are found in pockets in volcanic rocks, in the re-crystallised calcite of Burma, and in alluvium in Ceylon and Thailand.

RUBY. This stone, whose name comes from the Latin *rubeus,* is the most sought-after of precious stones. Its rich colour, due to pleochroism, is a mixture of purple red and a red lightly tinged with orange, which changes in intensity as the angle of the stone is changed. The so-called 'pigeon's blood' rubies are the rarest, and stones of more than 10 carats are exceptional and command fabulous prices. Even in the 16th century, the ruby was worth twice as much as the emerald, and eight times more than the diamond. The finest stones come from Mogok in Burma where they are found in beds of cipolin interlaid with gneiss. The two largest stones found since 1890 weighed respectively 400 and 304 carats uncut. Some valuable rubies are also found, together with sapphires, in alluvial deposits in Ceylon. The

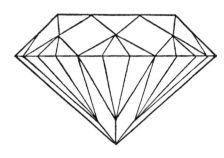
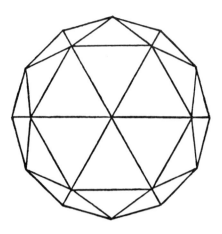
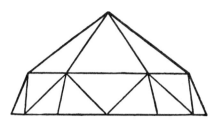

Left to right: the Antwerp cut, very effective on smaller stones since it leaves a large table without sacrificing the brilliance of the stone; and the Highlight cut, in which the number of facets has been increased to 68. Above: the Rose cut, for diamonds which are rather shallow

two largest cut rubies from Ceylon are both star rubies, and belong to American collections: the 'Rosser', of 138.7 carats, and the 'De Long Star', of 100 carats. Other countries producing rubies include Thailand, Cambodia, Tanzania and Kenya.

SAPPHIRE. The name is eastern, and in Greek it is *sappheiros*. Like the ruby, the sapphire has been known for a very long time; less rare, it was particularly in fashion throughout the Middle Ages. The best sapphires are pure blue or indigo; the slightest green component in the dichroic colour reduces the value of the stone considerably. Very large crystals, at least one as heavy as 20 kg, have been found. The choicest sapphires come (or came) from Burma and Kashmir; Ceylon produces stones whose colour ranges from a bright to a light blue, and others which can be pink, mauve, green, yellow or brown. Others come from Australia (deep blue and blue-black), Cambodia, Thailand (bright blue to blue-black, yellow and brown) and Tanzania.

HEMATITE. Iron oxide (trigonal). Known for thousands of years, hematite is used at the present day for inexpensive jewelry, on account of its fine metallic sheen, ranging from black to steel-grey. It is a common mineral, found in many different types of deposit. The finest crystals come from Brazil and the island of Elba.

QUARTZ. Silicon oxide (trigonal). One of the first minerals employed by prehistoric man, it exhibits a wide diversity of appearance. These have many different names, such as rock crystal (colourless), amethyst (violet), citrine (yellow), as well as rose, blue, smoky and milky quartz, all of which are crystalline forms; aventurine contains sparkling scales of brown mica, and other stones contain needle-like crystals of tourmaline or rutile (Venus' hair stone). Tiger's eye contains crocidolite, and can be old gold or blue, chatoyant (iridescent) or opaque. So-called cryptocrystalline quartz contains microscopic crystals and is known in many different forms with the general name of chalcedony: different chalcedonies can be red (cornelian), apple green

(chrysoprase), dark green with white or yellowish spots (plasma), brownish red (sard) or dark green with red spots (bloodstone or heliotrope); white, blue and grey forms are also common. Agate is a chalcedony banded in differently-coloured concentric zones. Onyx is agate with alternate black and white bands, either parallel or concentric. Sardonyx has alternate red-brown and white bands; moss agate contains red and green inclusions with a leafy look.

Jaspers are chalcedonies containing as much as 25 per cent of impurity, and with a wide variety of colour. The red spots in bloodstone are of jasper.

Quartz is one of the most widespread of minerals: it is found in the acid igneous rocks, in pegmatites, in hydrothermal lodes, and in crystalline schists; chalcedonies are of secondary origin, being found as crusts, as concretions in the sources of thermal springs, or as amygdules in basic volcanic rocks. Numerous illustrations in the colour pages of this book show the many forms in which quartz can be found.

OPAL. A hydrated form of silicon oxide, with an amorphous structure. One of the most beautiful of gems, opal is translucent and bathed in a milky light – 'opalescence' – shot with lively spectral colours, due to the many changes of refractive index produced by thin layers of stone and air, according to the angle of cross-section. The finest opals are found in Australia, Hungary and Mexico (the Mexican fire opal has an orange or red colour); they are found as nodules or incrustations in volcanic rocks such as andesite or trachyte.

Carbonates

SMITHSONITE. Zinc carbonate (trigonal). Certain crystals, which can be pink, yellow or green, may be cut and facetted, but they are not very brilliant stones; on the other hand, the superb translucent blue-turquoise makes very beautiful cabochons. Smithsonite, which is rarely of gemstone quality, can be found in weathered parts of zinc ores, or as substitution masses in limestone.

9

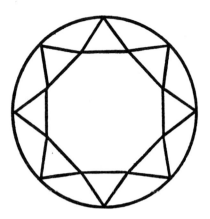 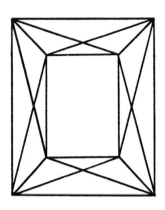 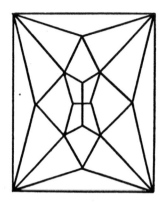

RHODOCHROSITE. Manganese carbonate (trigonal). Widely used at the present time as red masses ribbed with lighter veins. It can be found with various manganese ores and in certain substitution deposits in limestone.

AZURITE. Copper carbonate (monoclinic). A beautiful deep blue stone. Complexes of azurite and malachite are particularly sought after because of the rich contrasts of colour. The mineral is found in upper copper levels.

MALACHITE. Copper carbonate (monoclinic). A stone known since ancient times. The pieces employed for ornament are of a rich green with zones of lighter colour, and very beautiful objects can be shaped from this stone. It is widespread (large quantities occur in Siberia and Katanga) and is generally found together with azurite in the upper levels of copper deposits.

Phosphates

BRAZILIANITE. Sodium aluminium phosphate (monoclinic). This is one of the modern gems, having been described for the first time in 1945. Beautiful transparent green-yellow crystals are found in the pegmatites of Conselheira, Brazil; and the mineral also occurs in the USA.

APATITE. Calcium phosphate containing fluoride and chloride (hexagonal). Quite widespread, apatite is found in hydrothermal lodes, igneous and metamorphic rocks as crystals that can be colourless, yellow, green, pink or violet.

VARISCITE. Hydrated aluminium phosphate (orthorhombic). Also known as Utahlite, it occurs as compact masses of opaque greenish blue, with veins of brown.

TURQUOISE. Hydrated copper aluminium phosphate. A gem known (and artificially imitated) from the earliest times, turquoise is of an incomparable colour, to which it has given its own name; it is sometimes veined with black.

Its occurrence in large pieces has allowed the manufacture of costly objects. A rare mineral, it is of secondary formation, occurring in desert regions. The Egyptians mined it on Sinai, the Persians at Khorassan, and it was also worked by the Maya, the Incas and the Chimu.

Silicates

PHENAKITE. Beryllium orthosilicate (trigonal). Found in crystalline form – colourless, pale pink or yellowish – in pegmatites, granites and crystalline schists; the stones are valued by collectors of rare gems.

OLIVINE. Iron magnesium orthosilicate (orthorhombic). The name is often wrongly applied in English to green demantoid garnet. The gem variety of iron magnesium silicate is usually called peridot, and the name chrysolite, formerly applied to the yellowish-green variety of this stone, is better avoided. In ancient times, peridot was confused with topaz; olivine is a widespread mineral, but the gemstones, which may be found in very basic rocks, are becoming rare.

GARNET. This group of complex silicates, crystallising in the cubic system, forms an interesting family of gems. Pyrope (magnesium aluminium silicate) is of a good red colour, and is often known as Cape Ruby or Arizona Ruby; it is found in igneous rocks such as peridotites, kimberlite or serpentine. Almandine (iron aluminium silicate) is probably the 'crusaders' carbuncle'; it is deep red, and is found in gneiss and micaschist. Spessartite (manganese aluminium silicate) is orange-red or brown; it is rare, and is found in granites, pegmatites and rhyolites. Grossular garnet (calcium aluminium silicate), which may be brownish yellow (cinnamon-stone), reddish-orange (jacinth), green ('Transvaal jade') or other colours, is found in the metamorphic limestones. The most sought-after, demantoid garnet or 'olivine', is a variety of andradite (calcium iron silicate); it is green and, like the diamond, shows brilliant refraction colours. It is found in the contact

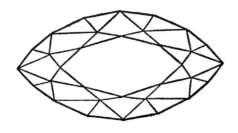

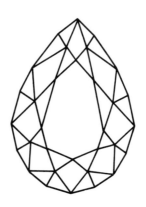

Other conventional styles of diamond cutting for various jewelry uses, or where the shape of the rough stone does not allow for brilliant cutting: marquise, pendeloque and briolette

zones of metamorphic strata, serpentine and chlorite schist, in the Urals and in Italy. Uvarovite (calcium chromium silicate) also comes from Russia. It is bright green, often opaque, and occurs in chromium-bearing serpentine and metamorphic limestones.

ZIRCON. Zirconium orthosilicate (tetragonal). The 'normal' or 'high' type occurs in a wide range of colours: yellow, light green, blue and red – the last is sometimes known as hyacinth. The 'low' type, in which the crystalline structure is almost completely broken down into an amorphous state, is greenish in colour. Stones of this type, which are found mostly in Ceylon, can be converted to the 'normal' crystalline type by prolonged heating. Zircons are found in acid igneous rocks, pegmatites and nephelinic syenites.

EUCLASE. Beryllium aluminium subsilicate (monoclinic). This stone has become so rare that many collectors prefer to keep it uncut. Pale green, pale blue or colourless, it is sometimes found, in a few localities, in pegmatites.

ANDALUSITE. Aluminium subsilicate (orthorhombic). Sometimes occurs as fine green or red-brown stones, with changing tones, in gneiss, micaschists and pegmatites.

KYANITE. Aluminium subsilicate (triclinic). Sometimes found in gneiss or micaschists, it is a fine sky-blue or blue-green.

TOPAZ. Aluminium fluoro-silicate (orthorhombic). Occurs as large fine stones, which may be colourless, blue, yellow or orange; pink stones are almost always produced by 'firing', a heat treatment that changes the colour. In ancient times the topaz was frequently confused with the peridot, and it is still sometimes confused with the citrine (a fired citrine is an amethyst whose colour has been changed to yellow-orange by heat treatment). Topaz occurs in acid igneous rocks in Brazil, Siberia and the USA, sometimes as crystals of more than 100 kilograms.

SPHENE (Titanite). Calcium titanium subsilicate (monoclinic). Well-cut stones, which can be yellowish-green or pinkish-brown, possessing a sharply-coloured brilliance; they occur in igneous or metamorphic rocks in Switzerland, Mexico and Burma.

DUMORTIERITE. Aluminium boron hydroxysilicate (orthorhombic). This stone, which occurs particularly in California, Arizona and Nevada, is increasingly used in ornament for its fine blue-violet colour. It is a metamorphic mineral found in association with acid rocks or in seams of quartz.

ZOISITE. Calcium aluminium hydroxysilicate (orthorhombic). Rose-red, green or brown, this stone occurs in igneous rocks with plagioclase feldspar, or in crystalline schists.

PREHNITE. Calcium aluminium acid silicate (orthorhombic). Green, like jade, or with a grey or yellowish tinge. A mineral of secondary origin, it is found in granites, gneiss, micaschists and basic volcanic rocks in France, the USA and Australia.

BENITOITE. Barium titanium silicate (trigonal). A rare gem very like a sapphire; stones heavier than three carats can command high prices. Benitoite occurs at San Benito in California.

BERYL. Beryllium aluminium metasilicate (hexagonal). While some crystalline stones can weigh as much as 100 tons, gem quality stones, with delicate transparent colours, are rare. The emerald differs from other beryls in its deep green colour, and has given its name to that luminous richness so sought after since ancient times. Aquamarine is blue to blue-green, morganite is pink, heliodor is golden yellow; there are also colourless, pale green and yellowish-green beryls. Gems are found in pegmatites, and adjacent to granites, particularly in zones of metamorphic limestones.

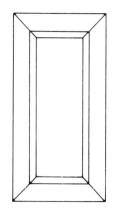 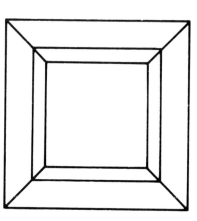 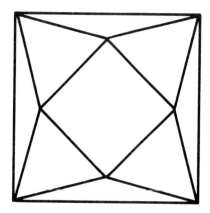

The EMERALD ('smaragdos' in Greek) is a precious stone that is rarely found entirely pure, and flaws reduce its value markedly when they are too apparent. Most emeralds come from Colombia, and the Indians of precolumbian America possessed enormous quantities. In the mine at Muzo, crystalline emeralds are found in association with hydrothermal penetration of complex bituminous deposits and igneous rock intrusions. Some beautiful stones have been found in the micaschists of Takowaya in the Urals; and in recent years Sandawana in Rhodesia has produced some pretty little emeralds. The stone is also found in Transvaal, India and Brazil. The oldest known mine is that of Sabara in Upper Egypt, which was worked by the Romans.

Aquamarine, morganite, heliodor and the other light-coloured stones are produced principally by Brazil, in the regions of Minas Gerais and Bahia, and crystals weighing sometimes 20 kilos or more have allowed the cutting of very large stones. From the Urals come aquamarines of a particularly beautiful blue; from Madagascar, light pink to violet-pink morganites. Several African sources produce fine beryls, particularly Mozambique, which is also renowned for its tourmalines.

IOLITE, also known as cordierite. Magnesium iron alumino-silicate (orthorhombic). A good blue stone, strongly pleochroic (deep blue/grey-blue/grey-yellow). It is found in certain volcanic rocks and lavas, and in some metamorphic rocks.

TOURMALINE. Complex borosilicate (trigonal). Elbaite (lithium-containing tourmaline) provides stones of marvellous colours; the range extends from pale pink, yellowish-brown, green, to greenish-blue. Some crystals are two-coloured. Rubellite is from pink to violet-red, and good stones are ranked very highly. Indicolite is dark blue or blue-green.

DRAVITE (tourmaline containing magnesium) is brown, sometimes with a yellowish tinge. Schorl, which contains iron, is black.

DIOPTASE. Copper acid silicate (trigonal). Always a very beautiful deep emerald-green. Much sought after by collectors, this mineral occurs in the weathering zone of certain copper deposits.

CHRYSOCOLLA. A hydrous copper silicate, with an amorphous structure. Turquoise-blue or green, with a glazed appearance, it is found in weathered copper deposits.

DIOPSIDE. Calcium magnesium metasilicate (monoclinic). Green or yellowish-green, sometimes white or brown. 'Violane' is opaque violet-blue. A variety of diopside, black in colour because of the presence of fine layers of magnetite, shows a fine four-rayed asterism. Diopside occurs in metamorphic rocks.

SPODUMENE. Lithium aluminium metasilicate (monoclinic). Sometimes occurs in fine crystals with delicate colours from yellow to pale green. Kunzite, first discovered near San Diego in California, is rose-coloured; hiddenite, from North Carolina, is grass-green. Spodumenes, which are not as valuable as beryls of the corresponding colours, occur in granites and pegmatites.

JADE. A name given to a group of silicates with an opaque, waxy, microcrystalline structure. There are two minerals which comprise 'true jade': jadeite, sodium aluminium silicate (monoclinic) and nephrite, a complex hydrous silicate containing calcium, magnesium and iron (monoclinic), and closely related chemically and geologically to asbestos. Jadeite can be white, green, pink, mauve or brown; particularly sought after is the emerald-green variety, 'Imperial jade', which may be found in thin seams in serpentine rocks. Nephrite can be white, grey, a wide range of greens, sometimes pink; it also is found in serpentine rocks, or in metamorphic schists. Chloromelanite is a variety of jadeite which is nearly black due to the inclusion of iron; chromojadeite contains chromium. Jades were worked by neolithic man, and in China beautiful objects have been made in this material for over 4,000 years.

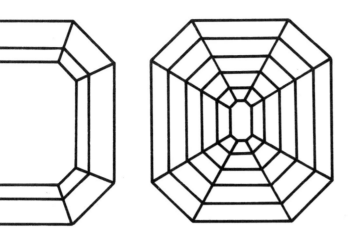

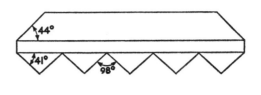

More conventional styles of gem cutting. From left to right: baguette, square, fancy star, trap or step cut (top plan), trap cut (base plan), and the profile or Princess cut. The purpose of this last is to provide diamonds which appear large as far as the table is concerned, but which do not require much depth of stone

RHODONITE. Manganese metasilicate (triclinic). A stone with a good pinkish-red colour, it is found in some iron and manganese deposits; the most famous is at Franklin Furnace in New Jersey.

ANTIGORITE. Magnesium silicate (monoclinic). Also known as serpentine, antigorite is a green stone resulting from the weathering of magnesium silicates, which has been used in imitation of jade.

FELDSPARS. A group of minerals which (as a group) is the most common of all – some five times as common as quartz. Orthoclase (monoclinic) and microcline (triclinic) are aluminium potassium silicate; oligoclase (triclinic) and labradorite (triclinic) replace the potassium with varying amounts of sodium and calcium. Orthoclase is colourless or yellow; moonstone is milky-white with a silvery opalescence. Microcline has a fine bright green form known as Amazon stone; now discovered most frequently at Pike's Peak in Colorado, it has been known since the earliest times, being found in syenites, granites and pegmatites.
  Oligoclase is known as sunstone or aventurine, and has a spangled brown colour due to the inclusion of flakes of hematite or geothite. Labradorite, which occurs in gabbros, is grey-blue to blackish blue or green, with brilliantly coloured iridescence.

SODALITE. A complex sodium silicate containing chloride (cubic). It is found in syenites and soda lavas, and the beautiful deep-blue crystals are increasingly employed in ornamentation.

LAZURITE. A complex aluminium silicate (cubic). A metamorphic mineral which is a very beautiful blue; it is one of the chief constituents of lapis-lazuli, and the crystals can be cabochon cut.

LAPIS LAZULI. A rock formed of several minerals, principally lazurite (together with other cubic system minerals such as sodalite and hauynite) and calcite or pyrites. Known and sought out for at least 6,000 years because of its rich blue colour, lapis lazuli occurs rarely in masses of any importance. The oldest known source is in Afghanistan, where the mineral occurs in a marble inclusion in a metamorphic rock. Other localities in which lapis lazuli suitable for ornamentation is found include a site near Lake Baikal in Russia, the province of Coquimbo in Chile, and California.

Non-crystalline and organic minerals

AMBER. A fossil resin, yellow to yellowish-brown, greenish yellow or reddish; it becomes electrically-charged on rubbing, and burns with a pleasant smell. It is notable for its very low density, being only slightly heavier than water.

JET. A fossilised wood related to coal; it was particularly popular during the last century for the fine black sheen it revealed on polishing.

TEKTITE. A naturally-occurring glass, possibly of meteoric origin; dark green or blue specimens are used in jewelry under the name of moldavite. It is found in recent Tertiary rocks and on the plains of central Europe, Australia and southeast Asia.

OBSIDIAN. A dark-brown or black volcanic glass, sometimes with fine chatoyancy. The best obsidians came from Mexico, where they were magnificently worked by the Aztecs. Well-known among the ancient peoples of the east, obsidian was also valued in Kenya and Abyssinia during the middle and upper Paleolithic for the manufacture of everyday objects.

CORAL. The chalky skeleton of the coral polyps (colonies of tiny animals which proliferate in temperate and warm

Mohs scale of hardness	
Talc	1
Gypsum	2
Fingernail	*about* 2½
Calcite	3
Copper coin	*about* 3
Fluorspar	4
Apatite	5
Window glass	*about* 5½
Feldspar	6
Knife blade	*about* 6
Quartz	7
Topaz	8
Corundum	9
Diamond	10

The numbers in this scale do not represent equal increases in degrees of hardness: the ten minerals were selected in a range of hardness, so that each will scratch any with a lower number in the scale but will not scratch any with a higher number

seas at depths between 50 and 200 metres). Rose-coloured and red corals have been used for a very long time in ornament, and statuettes carved from large pieces of coral can be highly valued.

PEARLS. Roughly concentric accretions of an organic substance, conchiolin, and calcium carbonate in the crystalline form known as aragonite. The best pearls are spherical, although they can also be of the irregular shape known as 'baroque'; they occur in certain molluscs of the sea or fresh water. Sought after since the most ancient times, pearls have a particular lustre of their own, whose iridescent nuances range from pink to yellow, from bluish to palest green, with an infinite range of intermediate shades including white. There are blue, black and pink pearls, but the highest-valued are from the salt-water molluscs *Meleagrina*. Cultured pearls are made by the artificial insertion of tiny balls of mother-of-pearl into the tissues of oysters; produced on an industrial scale, they are very much less valuable than natural pearls ('fine pearls'), whose price can rise greatly with size, eventually reaching a level comparable with that of precious stones. Principal pearl-fishing localities are in the Persian Gulf, the Gulf of Mexico, Ceylon, northwest coast of Australia and numerous islands in the Pacific.

False stones

Counterfeit gems can be divided into three principal groups: glasses ('paste' or 'strass'), synthetic gems and doublets.

GLASSES. The pastes made by the ancient Egyptians have given birth to two distinct techniques: the art of enamelling, a marvellous decorative form of which Byzantium, the middle Ages and the Renaissance have left us so many beautiful examples; and the glass industry, whose greatest improvements were in Roman times with the production of transparent coloured glass, and at the beginning of the eighteenth century with the manufacture of lead glasses with brilliant coloured scintillation.

All glasses can be readily recognised, since they have none of the properties of the gems whose colour they imitate: in particular, they frequently contain minute air bubbles very different in shape and attractiveness from the inclusions generally found in gems.

SYNTHETIC GEMS. Made on an industrial scale like other chemical products, these artificial stones (which should always be sold as such) bear the name of the mineral species which they resemble because they have an identical atomic structure and a near (but not always identical) chemical composition. The first commercial exploitation of the false gems began at the end of the last century; with the notable exception of strontium titanate (fabulite), which resembles diamond and is very expensive, the stones are seldom of any value. They can be recognised by the slight divergences that can be observed between their properties and those of the stones they resemble, and by the differences in their growth, the flaws and inclusions, due to the very different physico-chemical conditions in which they were formed.

DOUBLETS. Easily detected, these are compsite stones made up of two or sometimes three pieces (in which case the stone is called a triplet) cemented together with a transparent cement to produce a larger stone. There are various combinations: gem on gem, gem on glass, gem on synthetic stone, etc. As in the previous cases, these stones are of very little value.

Properties of some gemstones

	Density	Hardness	Refractive indices
Amber	1.05 to 1.11	2 to 2.5	1.54
Andalusite	3.2	7.5	1.64 and 1.69
Antigorite	2.36 to 2.55	2 to 4	1.49 to 1.57
Apatite	3.1 to 3.2	5	1.62 and 1.66
Azurite	3.8	3.5	
Benitoite	3.65	6.5	1.76 and 1.80
Beryl	2.65 to 2.88	7.5 to 8	1.56 to 1.60
Brazilianite	2.98	5.5	1.60 and 1.62
Chalcopyrite	4.2	4	
Cordierite	2.60 to 2.65	7 to 7.5	1.53 and 1.60
Corundum	3.96 to 4.10	9	1.76 and 1.77
Chrysoberyl	3.7	8.5	1.74 and 1.75
Chrysocolla	2 to 2.4	2 to 4	1.46 to 1.57
Diamond	3.50 to 3.54	10	2.417
Diopside	3.2 to 3.4	5 to 6	1.66 to 1.69
Dioptase	3.3	5	1.65 and 1.70
Dumortierite	3.25 to 3.35	7	1.66 and 1.69
Euclase	3.1	7.5	1.65 and 1.67
Fluorite	3.18	4	1.44
Garnets	3.60 to 4.10	6.5 to 7.5	1.74 to 1.89
Hematite	5 to 5.5	6	
Jadeite	3.4	6.5 to 7	1.65 and 1.67
Kyanite	3.55 to 3.65	4 to 7	1.71 and 1.73
Labradorite	2.70	6 to 6.5	1.55 and 1.56
Lapis Lazuli	2.4 to 2.9	6	
Malachite	4	3.5 to 4	
Microcline	2.55 to 2.60	6	1.51 and 1.52
Nephrite	2.9 to 3.2	5 to 6	1.60 to 1.64
Obsidian	2.4 to 2.6	5 to 5.5	1.50
Oligoclase	2.64 to 2.67	6 to 6.5	1.52 and 1.53
Olivine	3.27 to 3.40	6.5 to 7	1.63 to 1.69
Opal	2 to 2.15	5 to 6	1.43 to 1.46
Orthose	2.56	6	1.52 and 1.53
Phenakite	3	7.5 to 8	1.65 and 1.67
Prehnite	2.8 to 2.9	6 to 6.5	1.62 and 1.65
Quartz	2.65	7	1.54 and 1.55
Rhodocrosite	3.7	4	1.59 and 1.81
Rhodonite	3.4 to 3.6	5.5 to 6.5	1.72 and 1.73
Smithsonite	4.4	5	1.62 and 1.85
Sodalite	2.15 to 2.30	5.5 to 6	1.48
Sphene	3.4 to 3.55	5 to 5.5	1.90 to 2.05
Spinel	3.53 to 3.80	8	1.71 to 1.73
Spodumene	3.1 to 3.2	6.5 to 7	1.65 and 1.67
Tektite	2.3 to 2.4	5.5	1.49 to 1.51
Topaz	3.58	8	1.62 and 1.63
Turmaline	3 to 3.10	7 to 7.5	1.61 to 1.65
Turquoise	2.6 to 2.8	5 to 6	1.61 to 1.65
Variscite	2.6 to 2.9	3.5 to 4.5	1.56 to 1.59
Zircon	4.2 to 4.9	7 to 7.5	1.92 to 2.02
Zoisite	3.25 to 3.35	6 to 6.5	1.70 and 1.71

1 Modern lapidaries have inherited some of the cutting techniques employed by prehistoric man. Coarsely fashioned from flint, this weapon-tool, which could be held in the fist for many different uses, has been worked on both faces. Flint tools of this kind were used for nearly 500,000 years, from the Chellean to the Aurignacian ages. (French, author's collection). Above, a flint out of chalk, the most widely used material for the making of prehistoric tools

2 10,000 years of slow technical advance separate the manufacture of this jade neolithic axe and the eighteenth century Chinese necklace, in which the ornament and its chain were originally cut from a single piece of jade (School of Mining, Paris)

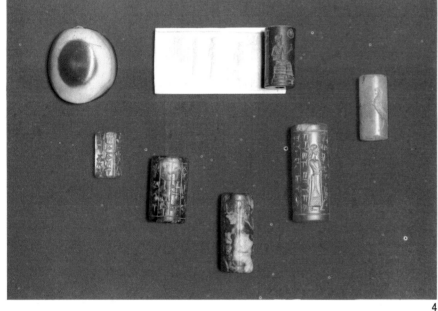

3   These two beautiful necklaces come from Mari (1500 BC). One is made up of very elegant pieces of cornelian, the other of different varieties of quartz circled with gold; the green stone is amazonite. (Louvre, Paris)

4   Upper left: a very interesting votive eye. Inscriptions engraved on the back endorse its attribution to a king of the third dynasty of Ur. The cylinder-seal in hematite is characteristic of the beginning of the second millenium BC; the seal in smoky quartz (left) is early Babylonian (1700 BC). The seal in bloodstone (deep green with red flecks) and the one in brown and white jasper date from 1400 BC. The last two are late Assyrian: in light pink and mauve chalcedony (800 BC) and white chalcedony (700 BC). (Louvre, Paris)

5   This beautiful counterweighted gold pectoral is an assembly of magical figurines, and each part has a precise symbolical significance. The divine barge carries a lapis lazuli scarab which bears a circular cornelian whose colour symbolises the sun low on the horizon; at each side dog-faced monkeys in turquoise, cornelian and amazonite bear on their heads a crescent moon surmounted by a disc. The counterweight is in cornelian, lapis lazuli and paste, and the rest of the necklace is decorated with paste. (Tutankhamen treasure, Cairo Museum)

The oldest of the styles from which the ancient art of Mexico developed, Olmec art, was established after 500 BC, and it is particularly well represented at La Venta, the source of this jade. (British Museum)

Among the innumerable jewels found at Susa this necklace of turquoises, cornelians and agates probably dates from the second millenium BC.

6

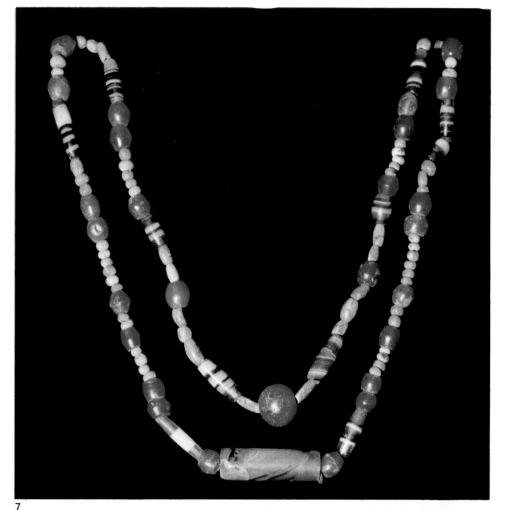

7

8

9

8 Greek art has left us innumerable engraved gems which represent the height of stonecutting. Worthy of Greek classical sculpture, this cameo on onyx (black and white banded agate) was found at Ephesus and dates from the fourth century BC. (Archeological Museum, Venice)

9 The first cutting of jade 'in the round' was in China, during the Chou dynasty, no doubt under the inspiration of surviving archaic bronze forms. This very beautiful disc (Pi type) was cut 500–300 BC. (Nelson Gallery of Art, Atkins Museum, Kansas City)

10 In Asia Minor, the cutting of flat seals, which had gradually been replaced by cylinders, returned to fashion after 1000 BC. The seals in white chalcedony and brown and white agate are Phoenician (800 BC); the seal in white-veined jasper (lower left) is also Phoenician (700 BC). The cylinder seal is Persian (600–500 BC). The seals (upper and lower right) in pale pink and brown chalcedony are Sassanid (400 AD). (Louvre, Paris)

11 Portrait of Alexander the Great. This marvellous relief (6 × 5 inches) is in ash-coloured chalcedony and is from the Hellenic or Roman era. Note the fineness of execution of the features and the curled hair beneath the Corinthian helmet. The setting is eighteenth century, of enamelled gold. (Bibliothèque Nationale, Paris)

12 This cup, shaped like a chalice without a foot, is in oriental sardonyx and is one of the greatest works of art of antiquity. Pride of the collection of Pope Paul II, and afterward of Lorenzo de Medici, the Magnificent, it has long belonged to the house of Farnese; hence its name the 'Farnese plate'. A gorgon's head is engraved on the underside; and in cameo at the bottom of the cup a sphinx and seven symbolic figures (the Nile, Horus, Isis, two nymphs and two figures representing summer winds) make up a striking greco-egyptian allegory. (Archeological Museum, Naples)

13 This necklace in gold and cornelian was found at Vulci, in Latium (400–300 BC). It shows what a refined taste for jewelry and gems the Etruscans possessed. (British Museum)

12

13

14

15

14 The 'Great Cameo', in five-layered sardonyx
12 × 10 inches, was engraved in Rome by Dioskorides
during the first years of the first century AD. Constantine
carried it to Constantinople with the imperial treasure,
and it remained there until Baudouin II offered it to
St Louis, king of France. It was placed in the treasury of
the Sainte-Chapelle, and there the demands of the
Catholic faith required this 'Triumph of Germanicus' to
become 'Joseph at the court of the Pharaohs'. Lent by
Philippe VI to the pope in 1379, the Great Cameo
returned to the Sainte-Chapelle in 1379, and remained
there until 1791, when it was deposited in the
Bibliothèque Nationale.

15 This Nubian ring was found in a royal tomb at
Ballana. It is of silver ornamented with an agate
surrounded by emeralds, amethysts and garnets.
(Cairo Museum)

16 Vases in precious stone were highly valued in Rome,
and this example in oriental sardonyx was the most
beautiful from that period possessed by Lorenzo de
Medici in his marvellous collection. It is engraved with his
flourish – LAU MED – and two thyrses (oriental
emblems) which indicate the oriental origin of this vase.
The mount is fifteenth century (Silver Museum, Florence)

16

17   18

17 A consular sceptre from fourth century Rome (total height 12½ inches, height of bust 3½ inches). This torso in ash-coloured chalcedony is probably that of Constantine the Great. It was transformed into a bishop's staff in the middle ages, and an inventory of 1480 records it in the Sainte-Chapelle. The drapery is modelled in silver-gilt, and the hands are silver. (Bibliothèque Nationale, Paris)

18 Jade figurine found at Oaxaca, Mexico. (American Museum of Natural History, New York)

19 This so-called cross of Berengario or cross of the realm is sixth century, made of gold encrusted with emeralds, garnets, sapphires, agate, pearls, and an old intaglioed amethyst suspended by the fine chain. The engraving on this amethyst, and the semi-cylindrical shape of the emeralds, show how many of the gems set in religious objects come originally from Roman jewelry. (Treasure of the Basilica of Monza)

20 This remarkable cup, engraved in relief with panels featuring animals, was carved from an enormous Persian turquoise. The rich gold mounting, set with enamels and gems, is Byzantine work of the tenth or eleventh century. It was given to the Venetian republic by Uzum Hassam, the Shah of Persia, in 1472. (Treasure of St Mark, Venice)

19

20

21

22

23

24

21 This rock crystal flagon, nearly 10 inches high, is of Fatimid manufacture and bears an inscription in sufic characters which enables us to attribute it to the era of the khalif El Aziz Billah (975–996). It was given to Thibaut, Count of Blois, by Ruggero I of Sicily, and was placed in the treasure of St Denis by Abbot Suger. (Louvre, Paris)

22 This large vase of red jasper (16 × 6 inches), with its spare and elegant line, was made in Venice in the eleventh or twelfth century. The flourish LAUR.MED indicates that it was an item in the Medici collection. The gilded silver mounting is attributed to Giusto da Firenze (late fifteenth century). (Silver Museum, Florence)

23 A statuette of a Chinese emperor in grey jade, Sung dynasty (960–1280). The small jades of this period are quite common, but the good pieces are, on the contrary, rare, particularly when they represent anything other than little ritual objects. (Gensburger, Paris)

24 Transportable altar of Emperor Henry II (18 × 14 × 5 inches). Made partly at Metz in 1000, and partly at Bamberg in 1030, this altar is made from an oak board surrounded by a wide oak frame, the whole covered with precious metal surrounding a central slab of rock crystal. The engraved surrounds are of gilded silver, their borders being decorated with sapphires, amethysts, emeralds, garnets, malachite and pearls; at the centre of the upper side is a ball of rock crystal, and at the bottom is a Byzantine intaglio representing St Paul. (Treasure of the Residenz Museum, Munich)

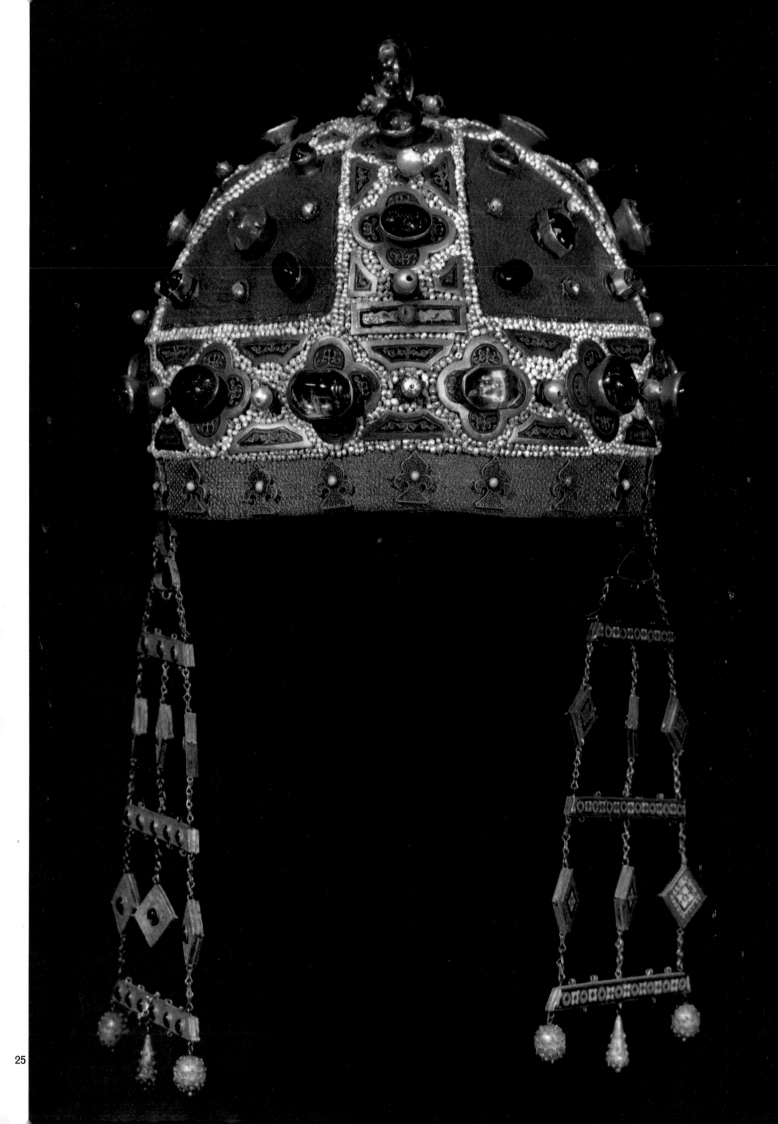

25 This magnificent thirteenth century crown was found on opening the tomb of Constance of Aragon; it is of enamelled gold enriched with sapphires, garnets, citrines, turquoise and pearls. Examination of these stones gives us some information on the lapidary techniques employed at this period: facet cutting was not yet adopted, and all the gems were polished into rough cabochons. The presence of a garnet covered with Arabic inscriptions confirms that at this date the difficult art of engraving on gems was still practised in the east. (Treasure of Palermo Cathedral)

26 This crown of the British royal house of Plantagenet was described in an inventory of 1399 as 'old goldware', and probably dates from the middle of the fourteenth century. Very distinctive, with its golden *fleurs de lys* decorated with rubies and sapphires and rosettes of pearls, it became part of the treasure of the Palatinate on the marriage of the daughter of Henry IV of England with Prince Louis III of Wittelsbach. (Treasure of the Residenz Museum, Munich)

27 The British Imperial State Crown and that of Elizabeth, the Queen Mother, bear some of the most famous gems of history. Mounted at the centre of the cross above the Imperial State Crown is the sapphire which adorned the finger of Edward the Confessor at his coronation in 1042 – the oldest jewel in the treasure of England. Lower, the splendid red spinel, which is known as the 'Black Prince's ruby', was described among the treasures of the King of Granada assassinated in 1367 by Peter the Cruel, King of Castille; this Peter presented the stone in token of his recognition of Edward Prince of Wales, the Black Prince. Later the life of Henry IV was saved by the solidity of this stone; it withstood the furious sword blow which the Duke of Alençon delivered to the king's helmet at the battle of Agincourt. Below the spinel, the large diamond is the second largest stone cut from the Cullinan; it weighs 317 carats

28 The largest diamond of the Queen Mother's crown is the Koh-i-Nor (mountain of light), a very beautiful Indian diamond slightly tinged with green. It was the most coveted diamond in history and the cause of pillage, torture and assassination. Its first known owner was the Rajah of Malwa; in 1850 the East India Company offered it to Queen Victoria. The two other large diamonds are (above) Cullinan III, of $94\frac{1}{2}$ carats; and Cullinan IV, of $63\frac{1}{2}$ carats. (Crown Jewels, Tower of London)

30

29 This very rich and beautiful reliquary, 12 inches high, is attributed to Hans Reiner and Hans Schleich (1585). Mounted on a chalcedony horse and armoured in enamelled gold, St George overthrows the dragon. The gilded silver pedestal is decorated with little ornaments and masks of enamelled gold; one can see the lozenged escutcheon of Bavaria supported by two lions, and the name of Maximilian I. The whole reliquary is enriched with numerous 'table-cut' diamonds, rubies, emeralds and pearls. (Treasure of the Residenz Museum, Munich)

30 Among the marvellous products of the Milan workshops during the sixteenth century, this great amphora, 20 inches high, is attributed to Annibale Fontana, who would have made it about 1575. This amphora is engraved with garlands of flowers, the arms of Bavaria, horses, fauns and winged satyrs. The handles with their sea goddesses, and the footrim, are in enamelled gold enriched with rubies and emeralds. (Treasure of the Residenz Museum, Munich)

31 This cameo portrait of Julius Caesar, in three-banded agate $2\frac{1}{4} \times 1\frac{3}{4}$ inches, was engraved in the sixteenth century, and demonstrates how at this time the art of engraved gems had again reached a point at which it could rival that of the ancient Greeks. The enamelled gold setting is enriched with four rubies and three diamonds. (Bibliothèque Nationale, Paris)

32 The art of mosaic saw a marked development during the seventeenth century, and this magnificent altar relief, a portrait of the donor Cosimo II de Medici, was made in 1619 by Giovanni Bilivert and Orazio Mochi. The admirable portrayal of the Grand Duke is greatly enriched by the enamelled gold of his robes and by nearly 260 diamonds strewn over them; and the rest of the mosaic is in agates, chalcedonies, jaspers (red, pink and blood) and lapis lazuli. It is probably the finest picture of this kind known. Size: 16 x 20 inches. (Silver Museum, Florence)

33 This covered cup in chalcedony ($10 \times 4\frac{3}{4}$ inches) was made in Italy in 1580, and is engraved with garlands. The mount and handles are in enamelled gold, decorated with rubies and pearls; and the handle of the cover, representing a negro, is in onyx and enamelled gold. It has been shown in the art collection since 1598, and in the treasure of Bavaria since 1637. (Treasure of the Residenz Museum, Munich)

31

32

33

34 This marvellous oval vase (over 16 inches high) is in lapis lazuli and is the work of Bernardo Buontalenti. Commissioned by Francesco de Medici and dating from 1583, it is (with the 'little ship' of Louis XIV in the Louvre) one of the two largest and most beautiful objects known to be made out of Afghanistan lapis lazuli. The enamelled gold mount is the work of Giovanni Bilivert. (Silver Museum, Florence)

35 Made from very fine German agate, this cup (8½ inches high) with a cover and base that reflect the shape of the bowl, once belonged to the Medicis; it was probably made in south Germany about 1650. The handle in the form of a soldier, and the bands decorated with arabesques which form the join of the cover, of the stem, and of the lower part, are all of enamelled gold. (Silver Museum, Florence)

36 This vase, which is of the same period as illustration 32, and in the same material, is only 10½ inches high. It is made of two pieces of lapis lazuli of different colour and texture, and its very elegant form is enhanced by the white enamelled swan beneath the lip. (Silver Museum, Florence)

37 The top of this square table is extremely elegant. Note particularly the refined taste with which the different coloured jaspers and marbles have been chosen, and the various tones of the lapis lazuli, (Prado, Madrid)

38 Already widely used for state furniture, the art of mosaic in precious stones developed considerably during the seventeenth and eighteenth centuries, and Italian craftsmen took work in many different royal workshops throughout Europe. This table is particularly rich, supported on the backs of four lions and bearing a design of garlands of flowers surrounding medallions of jasper, agate, lapis lazuli and amethyst; with a border encrusted with peridots, garnets and cornelians. (Prado, Madrid)

39 Among the collections of Louis XIV, this late-sixteenth century figure in bloodstone, of Christ at the pillar, is particularly admirable. The pillar is in rock crystal, and the pedestal in gold, decorated with figures in the round, bas reliefs, and enamels. Notice how the lapidary has adroitly used the flecks of red jasper to represent the trickles of blood after the flagellation. Height 9 inches. (Louvre, Paris)

38

39

40 A little head from ancient Mexico, provided with a setting in Italy during the seventeenth century. The mount is of enamelled gold, the two eyes are diamonds. (Silver Museum, Florence)

41 This graceful little cup in cornelian and agate (3¼ inches high) dates from the beginning of the seventeenth century. The mount is in enamelled gold. Note how the stem is formed by two clasped hands carved in the round. (Louvre, Paris)

42 This second little cup (less than 3 inches high) is in prase (massive green quartz) and dates from the same period. (Louvre, Paris)

43 An eighteenth century Turkish-made brooch, with diamonds, emeralds and pearls. (Topkapi Museum, Istanbul)

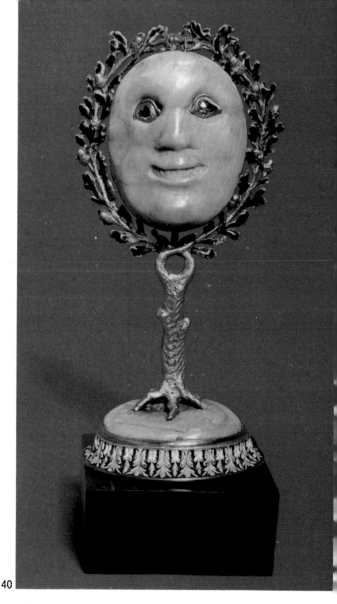

40

41   42

44 This magnificent dagger, its hilt made from three huge emeralds, is from the late seventeenth or early eighteenth century. The golden scabbard is very finely worked; the central decorative panel is in enamel, and the rest of the scabbard is studded with diamonds. (Topkapi Museum, Istanbul)

45 A late eighteenth century votive pendant, or possibly an ornament from a litter, made in gold mounted with diamonds, emeralds and pearls. The three objects on this page give some idea of the splendour of the existence of the Sultans of Turkey. (Topkapi Museum, Istanbul)

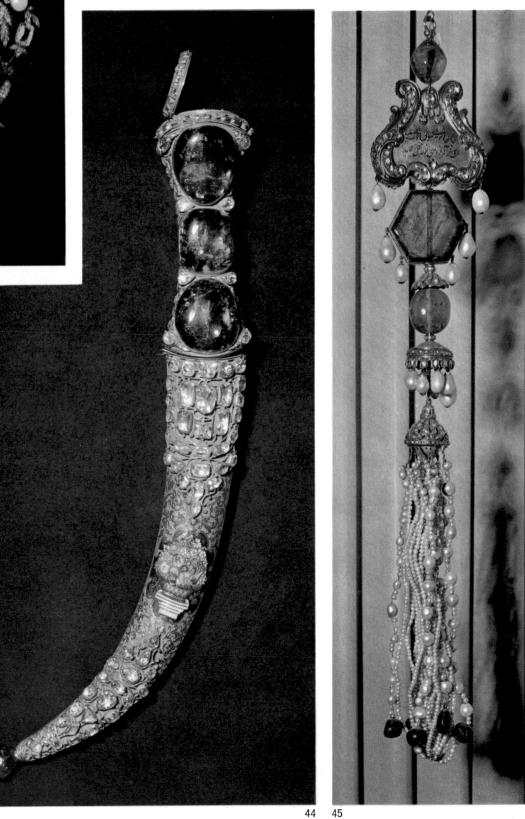

44   45

46

46 A Mogul vase of white jade, from the early eighteenth century. It is trellissed all over in fine gold mounted with rubies and emeralds. (Victoria & Albert Museum, London)

47 A fine example of Islamic art of the seventeenth century: a rock crystal flagon mounted in gold and studded with many different kinds of gem. (Topkapi Museum, Istanbul)

47

48 The delicate carving of this cornelian Buddha (late eighteenth century) enhances the intrinsic value of the stone. (Gensburger, Paris)

49 A swordhilt in jade, encrusted with fine gold and ornamented with rubies. The work is eighteenth century Mogul. (Victoria & Albert Museum)

50 A white jade cup of Chinese execution, made in the eighteenth century for the Persian court; its extremely thin walls are most delicately cut. It was subsequently offered to the Imperial collection in Peking: (Gensburger, Paris)

51 A Chinese triple inkstand in amber, eighteenth century. (Victoria & Albert Museum, London)

52 Steatite was widely used in China, and this nineteenth century object exemplifies the many possible uses of this ornamental mineral. (Author's collection)

53

54

53–54 These details from present-day mosaic work – part of a landscape, and a section of the border to a table – show that it can hold its own with that of past centuries. (Fiaschi, Florence)

55 Many small objects are nowadays made from gems and ornamental stones. This handful of little eggs in a chalcedony ashtray show how, even with modest means, it is possible to start a collection of gemstones

56–57 Raw diamonds; they show not only the simple cubic shape, but others derived from the cubic crystal system. (De Beers)

58 A 'pendeloque' cut diamond of 86 carats, once the property of the Sultans of Turkey. (Topkapi Museum, Istanbul)

59 A jonquil-coloured diamond. Diamonds with such pretty and clear colours are much sought after. (Van Cleef & Arpels)

60 The British royal sceptre bears the largest cut diamond in the world: Cullinan I, the largest piece (530.2 carats) of a stone which weighed 2,106 carats uncut, and which measured 4 x 2¼ inches. This stone was too big to be cut into a single gem, and it was split into nine large diamonds and 96 smaller pieces (see illustrations 42 and 43). (Crown Jewels, Tower of London)

58

59

61 Modern jewelry, in which the stones are held in an invisible setting by little grips, allows them to be seen in their full size and brilliance, as evidenced by this sumptuous set in diamonds and Burmese rubies. (Van Cleef & Arpels)

60

62 Alexandrite from Ceylon. It is emerald green by daylight, but red by artificial light. (School of Mining, Paris)

63 This enormous star ruby from Ceylon weighs 140 carats. Known as the 'Rosser Reeves' ruby, it is one of the largest in the world. (Smithsonian, Washington)

64 Many large sapphires are known. This Burmese star sapphire, weighing 330 carats, is known as the 'Star of Asia'. (Smithsonian, Washington)

65 Blue and yellow sapphires from Ceylon (left), and one from Kashmir. (Van Cleef & Arpels)

66 A crystal of ruby in calcite, from Mogok. (Sorbonne, Paris)

67 A rare 'pigeon's blood' ruby from Mogok. (Van Cleef & Arpels)

68 A 60 carat sapphire from Ceylon. Stones from this source are not usually as darkly coloured. (Grospiron, Paris)

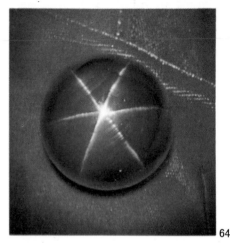

63

62

64

65

66

67

68

69

69 A geode of chalcedony from Germany. (Author's collection)

70 Madagascar quartz. (Author's collection)

71 Chrysoberyl: the raw crystal, and two yellow-green cut stones, and a cat's eye from Ceylon. (School of Mining, Paris)

72 More varieties of quartz: cornelian; green aventurine and black chatoyant aventurine; ashy chalcedony, chrysoprase and tiger's eye; Venus' hair stone and brown and white agate; and yellow chalcedony. (School of Mining, Paris)

73 Cut quartz: milky, yellow and orange-brown citrine, rock crystal, amethyst, rose, and smoky. (School of Mining, Paris)

70

72

71

73

49

74 Green zoisite is a rock in which rubies are often found at Longido in Tanzania; here the combination of the two colours has been used to excellent effect in this ornamental bird. (Compagnie Générale de Madagascar, Paris)

75–76 Oval dish made of agate from Uruguay: dog in smoky quartz from Brazil. (Bottega delle Pietre, Milan)

77 Lion in tiger's-eye from South Africa. (Bottega delle Pietre, Milan)

75

76

77

78 Further varieties of quartz: sard, 'flowered' jasper, bloodstone and moss agate. (School of Mining, Paris)

79 Two Australian opals and a Mexican fire opal. (Grospiron, Paris)

80 An opal elephant standing on raw opal, from Australia. (Author's collection)

81 Fire opal in its mother rock, Mexico. (School of Mining, Paris)

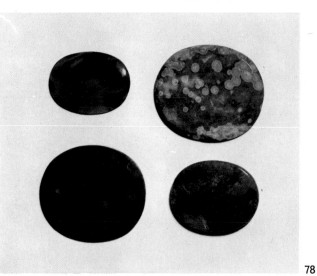

78

79

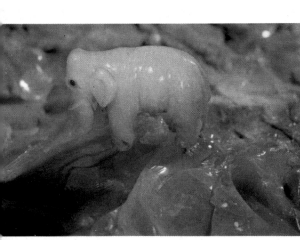

80

81

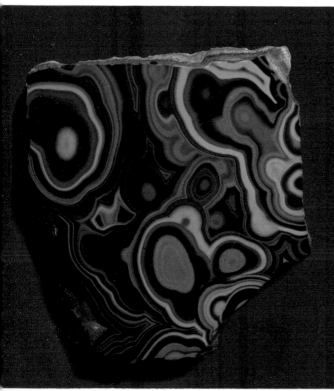

82 83

82 Malachite from Katanga. (Author's collection)

83 A delightful piece of Chinese work: a statuette cut in malachite. (Grospiron, Paris)

84 Rhodocrosite ('Inca rose') from Argentina, in piece and cut as a cabochon; variscite from Utah; yellow-green brazilianite, and a fine blue smithsonite from Laurium, Greece. (School of Mining, Paris)

84

85

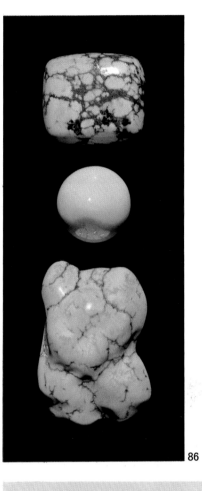

86

87

88

89

85 Spessartite garnet from Madagascar. (Compagnie Générale du Madagascar, Paris)

86 Turquoises from Persia; the black-veined stone is part of the mother rock or matrix. (Grospiron, Paris)

87 Peridots: an excellent crystal more than 2 × 1¼ inches, and three cut stones from Zebirget on the Red Sea. (School of Mining, Paris)

88 Green demantoid garnet from Siberia, spessartite from Brazil, and an almandine garnet. (Grospiron, Paris)

89 More garnets: an uncut crystal of almandine, green grossular ('Transvaal jade') and pink grossular from South Africa, a crystal of spessartite, and a cut Brazilian spessartite. (School of Mining, Paris)

90 Green prehnite from the USA, uncut and polished as a cabochon; and crude blue dumortierite from Madagascar and rose-red zoisite ('thulite')

91 Siamese zircons, light blue and blue. (Grospiron, Paris)

92 Three fine large topazes from Brazil. The colourless stone in the centre is of 616 carats. (Compagnie Générale du Madagascar, Paris)

93 A crystal of blue Siberian topaz in its mother rock. (School of Mining, Paris)

94 Nine topazes, three uncut crystals and six cut stones, which demonstrate the wide range of colours exhibited by this mineral. (School of Mining, Paris)

91

92

93　94

95 A necklace of Colombian emeralds. (Van Cleef & Arpels)

96 The step or trap cut is also known as the emerald cut, as exemplified in this fine Colombian stone. (Grospiron, Paris)

97 Another example of emerald as it occurs naturally with its mother rock. Muzo, Colombia (Sorbonne, Paris)

98 Emeralds: two engraved cabochons from India, and a polished cabochon from Colombia. (Grospiron, Paris)

99 Crystal emeralds in the mother rock. Muzo, Colombia. (School of Mining, Paris)

96

97

98   99

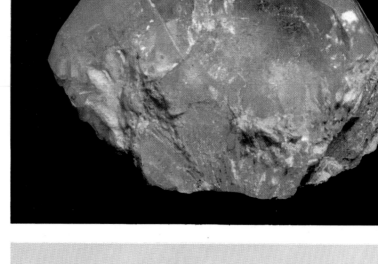

100

103

100 A fine large crystal, nearly 6 × 3 inches, of aquamarine from Governador Valadares, Brazil. (School of Mining, Paris)

101 An excellent crystal of morganite from Pala, California. (School of Mining, Paris)

102 Various coloured Brazilian beryls. (Compagnie Générale du Madagascar, Paris)

103 Brazilian morganite weighing 621 carats. (Compagnie Générale du Madagascar, Paris)

104 Rose beryl or morganite, with its mother rock, from the isle of Elba. (School of Mining, Paris)

105 Various coloured Madagascan beryls. Their cut, specially developed by P. Joz-Roland, won him the gold medal of the International Exhibition of Decorative Art in 1925

106 Red tourmaline, or rubellite, from Brazil. (Pitte, Paris)

107 Tourmalines in their mother rock, from San Pietro in Campo, on the island of Elba. (School of Mining, Paris)

105

106

107

108   109

108   Green Madagascan tourmaline. (Sorbonne, Paris)

109   Tourmaline from Pala, California. (Sorbonne, Paris)

110   Various coloured Brazilian tourmalines. (Joz-Roland, Paris)

110

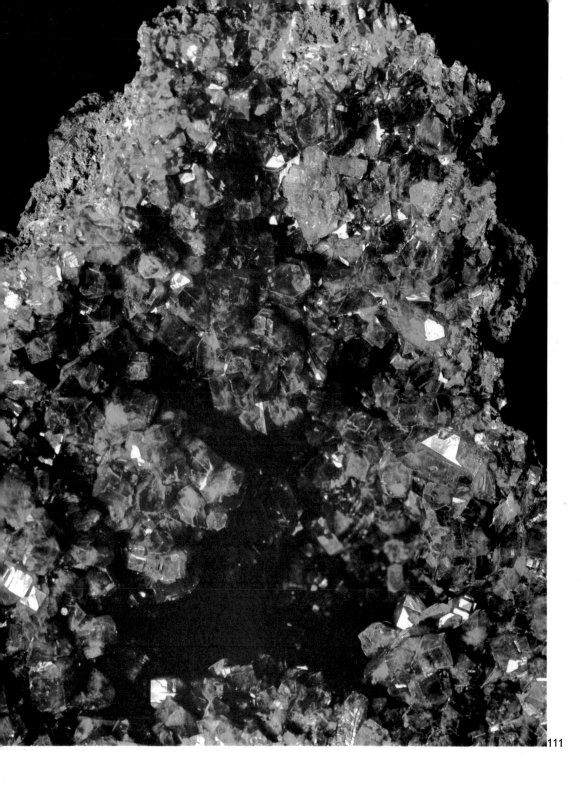

111

1 A magnificent geode filled with dioptase, from Reneville, ongo. The mass is nearly 7 × 6 inches. (School of Mining, Paris)

2 Chrysocolla in its raw state, and as a cabochon, from atanga; and a fine large cabochon of emerald-green dioptase om Reneville, over 1½ × 1 inch. (School of Mining, Paris)

112

11

114

113 Amazonite, the green microcline feldspar, from Colorado. This piece is 8 × 6 inches. (School of Mining, Paris)

114 Spodumenes: a beautifully-cut yellow-green faceted stone, bright green hiddenite from California, and pink kunzite from Brazil, in the crude and cut state. (School of Mining, Paris)

115 More rarely-used gems: willemite from the USA, a polished piece of friedelite, and kornerupine from Madagascar. (School of Mining, Paris)

115

116

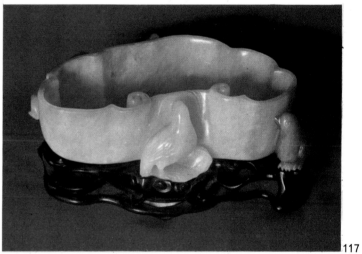

117

116 Chinese statuette in serpentine. (Grospiron, Paris)

117 Multicoloured jade, in green, mauve and yellow; this wonderful piece of Chinese work is of the eighteenth century. (Gensburger, Paris)

118 A bowl in Madagascan rhodonite. (Compagnie Générale du Madagascar, Paris)

118

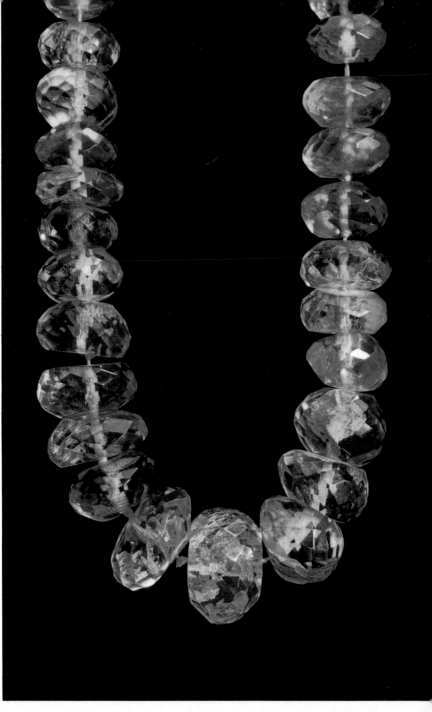

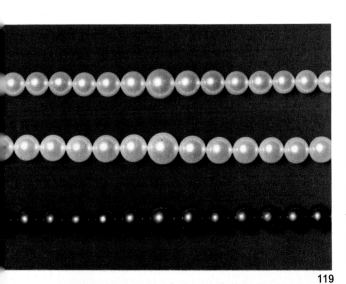

119

121

119, 121 Cultured pearls of different colours. (Grospiron, Paris)

120 Necklace of Baltic amber. (Compagnie Générale du Madagascar, Paris)

122 A salt cellar in Brazilian sodalite; and two pieces of lapis lazuli from Lake Baikal: the raw mineral and an oval polished disc.

122

123

24

125

126

23 Three microcline feldspars: oligoclase, or sunstone, with its bronze spangles; green amazonite from Brazil; and blue labradorite from Ceylon. Above, a polished piece of hypersthene, with its brown metalloid iridescence. (School of Mining, Paris)

24 A fine piece of German lapidary work: a statuette of a bison carved from Californian obsidian. (Compagnie Générale du Madagascar, Paris)

25 A beautiful yellow orthoclase from Itronguay, Madagascar, with a weight of 75 carats. (Compagnie Générale du Madagascar, Paris)

26 Moonstone from Ceylon. (Grospiron, Paris)

27 Natural tektite or moldavite, and a piece of the meteorite glass cut as a gem approximately 1 inch square. Below, a cabochon of black obsidian, and a piece of jet cut in facets. (School of Mining, Paris)

127

128 Two statuettes in coral, some excellent nineteenth century Chinese carving from the studio of prince Chou-en, Pekin. (Gensburger, Paris)

129 A branch of coral carved in the form of a dragon. (Grospiron, Paris)